EDUCATOR'S
QUICK REFERENCE GUIDE
to differentiation

by Laurie E. Westphal

WHAT IS DIFFERENTIATION?

DIFFERENTIATION is the way teachers anticipate students' needs in the classroom. Differentiation begins by determining what students need to know, understand, and do **(KUDs)** during any unit of instruction. It is important to understand that although strategies help teachers differentiate, differentiation is more than just strategies. Differentiation is a teaching lifestyle—a heuristic. As teachers begin to view their instruction using this lens, they can choose to differentiate their instruction through content, process, product, and environment according to students' readiness, interest, and learning preferences.

| **K** = know |

| **U** = understand |

| **D** = do |

Important Differentiation Principles and Strategies

CONTENT: What Students Learn	PROCESS: How Students Learn	PRODUCT: What Students Understand	ENVIRONMENT: Where Students Learn
How teachers share and instill concepts and skills the students need to know	How students process and make sense of the concepts and skills	How students show what they know and understand about the content learned	The setting or climate created in the classroom by both teachers and students
• Resources that match students' ability levels • Options that respect what students already know	• Activities at different levels of difficulty and support • Options addressing students' interests and preferences	• Varied opportunities for challenge and choice • Product choices are respectful of students' learning preferences	• Safe and positive environment that encourages expression of ideas • Allows for individual work preferences
Strategies Included in This Guide			
• Curriculum Compacting • Learning Contracts • Most Difficult First • Tiered Activities • Jigsaw	• Learning Contracts • Most Difficult First • Anchor Activities • RAFTs • Tiered Activities • Jigsaw • Flexible grouping	• Learning Contracts • RAFTs • Tiered Activities	Each strategy includes a "Making it Your Own" section; these options help teachers customize strategies and create a differentiated classroom climate

DIFFERENTIATION STEP 1: KUDs

KUDs (Tomlinson & Moon, 2013) is an acronym for know, understand, and do. Teachers use these three keywords before beginning any differentiated unit to determine student instructional expectations. KUDs:

- provide the basis for effectively differentiating the unit,
- focus teachers before beginning their planning and guide instruction during the unit, and
- allow teachers to confirm when students have mastered necessary skills and concepts.

Before beginning a new unit, determine what students will need to know **(K)**, understand **(U)**, and do **(D)** as the unit progresses. Record these ideas in a chart, and display this chart in the classroom so both students and teacher understand the expectations **(see Figure 1)**.

KNOW:
(Facts, people, dates, vocabulary, information)

Students will know the stages or processes of the water cycle.

UNDERSTAND:
(Generalizations, big ideas, concepts)

Students will understand how water is changed as it moves through the water cycle.

DO:
(Skills, levels of thinking, communication, strong verbs)

Students will write a story about the life and experiences of a raindrop as it moves through the water cycle.

FIGURE 1. Sample KUDs.

Heacox, D. (2017). *Making differentiation a habit: How to ensure success in academically diverse classrooms* (2nd ed., pp. 7–9). Minneapolis: MN: Free Spirit.

Narvaez, L., & Brimijoin, K. (2010). *Differentiation at work, K–5: Principles, lessons, and strategies* (pp. 20–34). Thousand Oaks, CA: Corwin Press.

Tomlinson, C. A., & Moon, T. R. (2013). *Assessment and student success in a differentiated classroom*. Alexandria, VA: ASCD.

CURRICULUM COMPACTING

Curriculum compacting (Reis & Renzulli, 1992) is a three-phase process in which teachers determine what students already know and provide them with quality alternate activities.

1 Name It
Define goals.

2 Prove It
Measure students' mastery.

3 Change It
Provide acceleration and enrichment.

Benefits

- Can be used at any grade level and with any content
- Can extend or enrich the current unit
- Provides challenge for students at their current ability and pace levels
- Increases motivation and success by offering choice and respecting students' prior knowledge

Design/Implementation

1. Identify the objectives or goals for the current unit **(KUDs)**.
2. **(a)** Identify the students who may benefit from compacting. **(b)** Select or create an appropriate pretest to evaluate the KUDs. **(c)** Determine mastery levels for the pretest. **(d)** Assess selected students the with pretest.
3. Provide acceleration or enrichment options for students who showed mastery on the pretest **(see Learning Contracts and Tiered Activities)**.

Making It Your Own

- Sources for identifying students who may benefit from compacting may include: standardized test results, class participation, previous tests, completed assignments.
- Consider different levels of pretest mastery. For example, 75% correct on the pretest may be enough for students to compact different aspects of the unit.

Reis, S., & Renzulli, J. (1992). Using curriculum compacting to challenge the above average. *Educational Leadership, 50*(2), 51–57.

Reis, S. M., Renzulli, J. S., & Burns, D. E. (2016). *Curriculum compacting: A guide to differentiating curriculum and instruction through enrichment and acceleration* (2nd ed.). Waco, TX: Prufrock Press.

Robinson, A., Shore, B. M., Enersen, D. L. (2007). *Best practices in gifted education: An evidence-based guide* (pp. 117–121). Waco, TX: Prufrock Press.

Sousa, D. A. (2009). *How the gifted brain learns* (2nd ed., pp. 50–51, 65–67). Thousand Oaks, CA: Corwin.

Tomlinson, C. A. (2001). *How to differentiate instruction in mixed-ability classrooms* (2nd ed., pp. 74–75). Alexandria, VA: ASCD.

Tomlinson, C. A. (2014). *The differentiated classroom: Responding to the needs of all learners* (2nd ed., p. 148). Alexandria, VA: ASCD.

Winebrenner, S., & Brulles, D. (2008). *The cluster grouping handbook: How to challenge gifted students and improve achievement for all* (pp. 84–115). Minneapolis, MN: Free Spirit.

LEARNING CONTRACTS

Learning contracts are agreements between teachers, students, and sometimes parents. These agreements include skills or objectives, and outline what students will learn in a predetermined amount of time during an instructional unit.

Benefits

- Can extend or enrich the current unit of study in any content area
- Allow students to become active participants in their own learning
- Manage classrooms with multiple ability levels
- Increase motivation, independence, and participation by allowing choice
- Address learning preferences and specific needs
- Encourage students to work at their own pace, helping them develop their planning, time management, and decision-making skills

> ❝ Allow students to become active participants in their own learning ❞

Design/Implementation

1. Determine the objectives, learning outcomes, or essential questions the students should be able to answer at the end of the unit (KUDs). This information will be used to design the contract.
2. Learning Contracts have flexible designs, but usually include certain components:
   a. **Tasks/Goals/Outcomes:** Provide a list of the tasks that will be accomplished, with a brief description of the expected outcome(s). Tasks may be nonnegotiable, optional, or a mix of both, depending on the design.
   b. **Resources:** Discuss the resources that students should or could use to complete their tasks. This section should consider availability of resources in class or at home.
   c. **Timeline:** Specify deadlines or checkpoints for completing the different tasks selected or indicated in the contract.
   d. **Assessment/Evaluation:** Indicate how each task will be evaluated. This component usually includes student-friendly checklists or rubrics.
   e. **The Agreement:** Outline the student's responsibilities during the execution of the contract. It includes the signature of the teacher, the student, and parent, if appropriate **(see Figure 2)**.

Name: _____ Date: _____

Basic Learning Contract

Activities I will complete: Due Date:
1.
2. **Tasks/Goals/Outcomes**   **Timeline**
3.

I will present my activities in the following way: _____

I plan to use the following resources: **Resources**
- Textbook
- Laptop
- Internet
- Library book
- Interviews

My work will be graded using: _____ *(Rubric attached, if appropriate)*
Assessment/Evaluation

By signing below, I agree that:
- I will stay on-task at all times and work quietly.
- I will follow directions and ask for help when I need it.
- I will complete my work neatly and turn it in on time.

Student's Signature: _____ **The Agreement** Date: _____
Teacher's Signature: _____ Date: _____

FIGURE 2. Sample learning contract.

Making It Your Own

- Start with smaller/shorter contracts (1–2 days) to introduce the management skills students will need for longer contracts.
- Contracts can take different forms, including charts, checklists, choice boards, or extension menus.
- Use contracts after curriculum compacting or to manage independent studies.
- Negotiate, allowing the students to have choice in activities placed on the contract.
- Students may need help setting realistic deadlines, and contracts may need to be revisited if students are struggling.
- Teachers may wish to include a statement of their responsibilities to the student as part of the agreement.

References/Additional Resources

Heacox, D. (2017). *Making differentiation a habit: How to ensure success in academically diverse classrooms* (2nd ed., pp. 54–67). Minneapolis: MN: Free Spirit.

Tomlinson, C. A. (2001). *How to differentiate instruction in mixed-ability classrooms* (2nd ed., p. 76). Alexandria, VA: ASCD.

Tomlinson, C. A. (2014). *The differentiated classroom: Responding to the needs of all learners* (2nd ed., pp. 139–144). Alexandria, VA: ASCD.

Westphal, L. E. (2016). *Differentiating instruction with menus: Math, grades 3–5* (2nd ed.). Waco, TX: Prufrock Press. (Note. See full series for grades K–2, 3–5, and 6–8 menus in each content area.)

Winebrenner, S. (2001). *Teaching gifted kids in the regular classroom* (Rev. ed., pp. 47–66). Minneapolis, MN: Free Spirit.

Winebrenner, S., & Brulles, D. (2008). *The cluster grouping handbook: How to challenge gifted students and improve achievement for all* (pp. 95–105). Minneapolis, MN: Free Spirit.

TIERED ACTIVITIES

Tiered activities allow the teacher to provide students with parallel learning tasks that are targeted just above their current ability level. Tiered activities can be designed based on student readiness, complexity, abstractness, interest, or learning preference.

Benefits

- Encourage reinforcement or extension of concepts
- Increase engagement and motivation as students feel successful
- Allow all students to progress and be appropriately challenged while learning the same content or objectives
- Assure that students understand the skills or objectives because content is presented at their level

Design/Implementation

1. Determine the objectives, ideas, and skills that are essential for students to understand in the content being studied **(KUDs)**.
2. Consider and confirm students' readiness, interests, and/or learning preferences. This may include the use of formative and summative assessments, and learning inventories.
3. Develop one activity that is high-interest, uses higher level thinking, and requires students to use the skills determined earlier in the KUDs.
4. Place this activity at an appropriate level on a tiered "ladder." The top rung of the ladder represents students who are highly skilled and already have a deep understanding of the content. The lowest rung represents students who lack the needed skills or understanding of the content.
5. Replicate the activity along the ladder, creating different versions of the activity. These versions may **(a)** be more or less difficult; **(b)** use different levels of resources; **(c)** focus on the concrete or the abstract; **(d)** be structured or open-ended; **(e)** allow students to show their learning through more familiar or more unfamiliar products; or **(f)** require less or more independence to complete them **(see Figure 3)**.
6. Once the tiered activities are created, match each student with an activity based on the considerations determined in step two.

Making It Your Own

- Teachers can select the appropriate number of tiers based on the different levels in his or her classroom. A more homogenous classroom may need just two tiers; a heterogeneous classroom may require up to five.
- Be sure to select appealing activities for all tiers and introduce the activities with equal interest and enthusiasm.
- Tiered activities should be designed to provide different work, not just more or less work for each tier.

Tier	Ability Levels	These Students May Require	Example
1	Lowest skills and understanding	◆ Less difficult reading sources with graphics ◆ Concrete activities and information ◆ Fewer steps to address the task ◆ The lowest levels of Bloom's taxonomy when working independently	Write a biography about your scientist. Use the event timeline to organize your ideas. Remember to answer the "5 Ws and an H" (Who, What, Where, When, Why, and How) in your biography.
2	On-level skills and understanding	◆ On-level reading sources, such as the textbook ◆ The opportunity to move from concrete to abstract concepts during the activity ◆ A mix of both closed and open-ended questions ◆ The opportunity for students to move through the different levels of Bloom's taxonomy while working independently	Write a biography about your scientist. Use your event timeline to organize your ideas. Your biography should provide evidence that supports why your scientist is considered famous.
3	Highest/advanced skills and understanding	◆ More complex and lengthy reading sources (other than the textbook) ◆ Abstract activities and information ◆ Open-ended questions ◆ The highest levels of Bloom's taxonomy when working independently, asking students to analyze, evaluate, and infer	Write a biography about your scientist. It must be written using a journal format, in which your scientist tells the story of his or her famous life through his or her own words.

FIGURE 3. Sample tiered activities (*Note.* Although it is not necessary to use a ladder when designing your tiered activities, creating a chart makes the tiers easier to visualize.)

References/Additional Resources

Eidson, C., Iseminger, B., & Taibbi, C. (2008). *Demystifying differentiation in elementary school: Tools, strategies, & activities to use NOW* (pp. 19–152). Marion, IL: Pieces of Learning.

Heacox, D. (2017). *Making differentiation a habit: How to ensure success in academically diverse classrooms* (2nd ed., pp. 81–105). Minneapolis: MN: Free Spirit.

Kingore, B. (2011). *Tiered learning stations in minutes! Increasing achievement, high-level thinking, and the joy of learning.* Austin, TX: PA.

Narvaez, L., & Brimijoin, K. (2010). *Differentiation at work, K–5: Principles, lessons, and strategies* (pp. 116–179). Thousand Oaks, CA: Corwin.

Sousa, D. A. (2009). *How the gifted brain learns* (2nd ed., 59, 81–82). Thousand Oaks, CA: Corwin.

Tomlinson, C. A. (2001). *How to differentiate instruction in mixed-ability classrooms* (2nd ed., pp. 34–50). Alexandria, VA: ASCD.

Tomlinson, C. A. (2014). *The differentiated classroom: Responding to the needs of all learners* (2nd ed., pp. 133–138). Alexandria, VA: ASCD.

MOST DIFFICULT FIRST

Most Difficult First (Winebrenner, 2001) is a basic form of compacting instruction. The teacher allows students to demonstrate mastery of a concept by having students complete the five most difficult problems of an assignment. If students can complete these problems, they participate in an alternate activity without having to complete the entire original assignment.

Benefits

- Facilitates a respectful atmosphere that acknowledges different ability levels
- Encourages critical thinking by allowing able students to work at a more complex level
- Averts boredom by allowing students to move to more appropriate challenges

Design/Implementation

1. Star or highlight the five most difficult questions, problems, or tasks on an assignment.
2. Give all students the opportunity to show mastery by independently completing the five starred items.
3. For students who demonstrate mastery, give full credit for the assignment and provide another appropriate activity covering the same content (see Anchor Activities and Learning Contracts).
4. For students who do not demonstrate mastery or need to ask for help while completing the five items, have them complete the entire assignment.

Making It Your Own

- Allow different levels of mastery. Rather than requiring perfection (5 out of 5), count four of the five items correct as credit for the assignment.
- Alter the number of problems highlighted. If the assignment or time is shorter, it may be appropriate to highlight just three.

Azzam, A. (2016). Six strategies for challenging gifted learners. *Education Update, 58*(4), 2–4.

Winebrenner, S., & Brulles, D. (2008). *The cluster grouping handbook: How to challenge gifted students and improve achievement for all* (pp. 91–95, 109). Minneapolis, MN: Free Spirit.

Winebrenner, S. (2001). *Teaching gifted kids in the regular classroom* (Rev. ed., pp. 35–38). Minneapolis, MN: Free Spirit.

FLEXIBLE GROUPING

Flexible grouping allows different grouping configurations during instruction, such as whole-class groupings, small groupings, partner groupings, or individual groupings.

Benefits

- Allows students to work with and learn from their peers in a supportive and appropriate setting
- Allows the teacher to differentiate instruction based on individual student needs, including academic, social, and emotional needs
- Encourages students to work independently and cooperatively, increasing responsibility and confidence

Design/Implementation

1. Identify the objectives or goals for the current unit (KUDs).
2. Determine the instructional considerations for the participating students. These considerations may include ability levels, background knowledge, interests, work habits, emotional needs, readiness, learning preferences, specific talents, and access to technology.
3. Create groupings. Students may be divided into individual, pair, triad, quad, "unequal," or whole-class groupings. These groupings may stay together for various lengths of time (10 minutes, a class period, a week, or longer). Ultimately, these groups must be flexible and dynamic—changing as students' needs and considerations change.
4. Share clear instructions, expectations, and outcomes for tasks the group(s) will complete.

Making It Your Own

- Teachers can consider using both homogenous (when wanting to move beyond current knowledge) and heterogeneous (when wanting to focus on relationship building and cooperation) groupings.
- Once students flow into and out of flexible groups, teachers can have fun with quick random groupings. For example, students could be grouped by birth month, types of shoes they are wearing, random card draw, or "clock partners." These quick groups can be effective for brainstorming, checking answers, or sharing questions about the instruction.

Ford, M. (2005). *Differentiation through flexible grouping: Successfully reaching all readers.* Naperville, IL: Learning Point Associates.

Hughes, L. (1999). Action research and practical inquiry: How can I meet the needs of the high-ability students within my regular education classroom? *Journal for the Education of the Gifted, 22,* 282–297.

Tomlinson, C. A. (2001). *How to differentiate instruction in mixed-ability classrooms* (2nd ed., pp. 23–26). Alexandria, VA: ASCD.

ANCHOR ACTIVITIES

Anchor activities are teacher-provided, content-based options for independent work when students have "downtime," such as after finishing an assignment, entering the classroom, or waiting for help during an activity.

Benefits

- Provide a strategy for dealing with unstructured or "ragged" time as students finish their classwork

- Maximize instructional time, providing ongoing options to further explore (or review) the content being studied

- Help facilitate independence as students select and complete activities they find meaningful

Design/Implementation

1
Determine important concepts or objectives for the current or upcoming units of study **(KUDs)**.

2
Based on this information, brainstorm enrichment or reinforcement activities for the unit(s). These activities should **(a)** be engaging and meaningful, not busy work; **(b)** be able to be completed independently; **(c)** provide varied levels of challenge; and **(d)** address different learning preferences **(see Figure 4)**.

3
Compile these activities and share them in a student-friendly, age-appropriate manner.

Making It Your Own

- Anchor activities may last a few minutes, a class period, or an entire semester.
- These activities can be shared in different ways, including printed lists, posters, bulletin board displays, and learning centers.
- Choose how to evaluate anchor activities depending on their use (e.g., choose not to grade these activities, or design rubrics based on the expected outcome of each activity).

After finishing an assignment in math, students could:

- Create their own word problem(s) to stump their classmates.
- Write a riddle for a certain number or mathematical function.
- Research a different number system (Egyptian, Arabic, etc.) and make a poster to explain the system. Include a math problem using this system.

FIGURE 4. Sample anchor activities.

Heacox, D. (2017). *Making differentiation a habit: How to ensure success in academically diverse classrooms* (2nd ed., pp. 121–126). Minneapolis: MN: Free Spirit.

Schlemmer, P., & Schlemmer, D. (2008). *Teaching beyond the test: Differentiated project-based learning in a standards-based age* (pp. 38–41). Minneapolis, MN: Free Spirit.

Tomlinson, C. A. (2001). *How to differentiate instruction in mixed-ability classrooms* (2nd ed., p. 35). Alexandria, VA: ASCD.

References/
Additional
Resources

RAFTs

RAFT (Santa, 1988) is an acronym for role, audience, format and topic. In this strategy, teachers provide students with a list of creative options requiring students to assume a role and create a product in a certain format, addressing a topic for a predetermined audience.

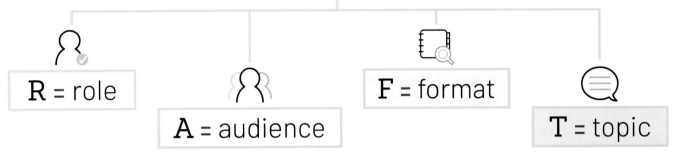

Role	Audience	Format	Topic
Who or what is the student as the writer? This can be a person or object and helps foster voice.	To whom is the student writing? This can be a person or object and helps determine content and foster style.	What format should the student use, or what product should he or she create? This helps students understand conventions of writing.	What is the student writing about and why? This helps the students focus on main idea and supporting details.
Examples: ◆ Journalist ◆ Soldier ◆ Plant's roots ◆ The letter A ◆ Cell's nucleus ◆ The president ◆ Student	Examples: ◆ Friend ◆ Family ◆ Plant's leaves ◆ Other vowels ◆ Mitochondria ◆ Self ◆ Math book	Examples: ◆ Poem ◆ Math problem ◆ Interview ◆ Political cartoon ◆ Lab report ◆ Advertisement ◆ Children's book	Examples: ◆ Relevant to current unit or time period ◆ Personal interest in the role, even if the role is inanimate ◆ Relevant scenario based on audience
The letter Y	Other vowels	Song	Can I be part of your group?

FIGURE 5. Sample RAFTs.

Benefits

- Encourage writing across the curriculum and are effective in all content areas
- Address student interests and learning preferences
- Foster creativity and critical thinking by asking students to analyze and consider the topic being studied in unique ways that often extend beyond classroom instruction
- Motivate and engage by offering students a choice of writing options

Design/Implementation

1. Determine the concepts and skills students will need to demonstrate **(KUDs)**.
2. Prepare a grid or table format with one of the RAFTs keywords at the top of each column **(see Figure 5)**.
3. Brainstorm items for each column: Roles for the writer to assume, Audiences to whom the student writes, Formats for the product, and Topics to address in the product.
4. Arrange each column so that by reading across a row, the students create a unique prompt. The example provides tips and examples for designing each column.

Making It Your Own

- More flexibility can be added by leaving a row blank at the bottom of the RAFT for students to brainstorm their own ideas for each column.
- A RAFT can be designed with one consistent column. For example, the topic column may be the same for the entire chart, with the other columns varying. This way, students write about the same topic but approaching it from different viewpoints.
- Alternative formats can be used for different learning preferences, including plays, commercials, or displays.
- RAFTs can be brainstormed and created by students. Students can brainstorm different roles, audiences, and formats. Be sure to confirm that the brainstormed options align with the curriculum objectives identified in the KUDs.

References/ Additional Resources

Groenke, S. L., & Puckett, R. (2006). Becoming environmentally literate citizens: Students use the RAFT writing strategy to address land development issues. *The Science Teacher, 73*(8), 22–27.

Heacox, D. (2017). *Making differentiation a habit: How to ensure success in academically diverse classrooms* (2nd ed., pp. 76–77). Minneapolis, MN: Free Spirit.

Narvaez, L., & Brimijoin, K. (2010). *Differentiation at work, K-5: Principles, lessons, and strategies* (pp. 116–179). Thousand Oaks, CA: Corwin.

Santa, C. (1988). *Content reading including study systems: Reading, writing and studying across the curriculum* (pp. 120–128). Dubuque, IA: Kendall/Hunt.

JIGSAW

Jigsaw (Aronson, 1978) is a cooperative activity consisting of "home groups" and "expert groups." Students leave their home group to join an expert group to learn a specific aspect of the content being studied. Students then return to their home group and share their expertise.

Benefits

- Encourages cooperative learning in "home groups" and "expert groups"
- Improves listening and communication skills
- Facilitates active learning and build students' confidence in the content
- Allows students to investigate their interests in the unit of study

Design/Implementation

1. Examine the content and resources for the upcoming unit or lesson. Determine the best way to break the content into topics or sections. Each section will be studied by an expert group **(see Figure 6)**.
2. Place students into heterogeneous home groups with the same number of members as expert groups. For example, if the content will be broken into four sections for study, each home group should have four members.
3. Each student will choose (or be assigned) an expert group based on his or her interests. Each home group should have one person participate in each expert group.
4. Students join their expert groups to discuss their assigned section. Expert group members should help each other understand the information and practice how they will present the information to their home groups.
5. Experts return to their home group and take turns sharing and teaching their home group about the section they studied.

Making It Your Own

- Home group members should be encouraged to take notes and ask questions while the expert is sharing.
- Expert groups can be given as much or as little leading information based on their abilities and readiness. Some groups may benefit from guiding questions, graphic organizers, charts, or materials written at different reading levels to help the processing. Other groups may benefit from being given resources to investigate the content and draw their conclusions for sharing.

Broken into five topics or sections, which will be expert groups.

Topic: Civil War				
Battles	Northern Life During the War	Southern Life During the War	Causes or Events Leading to War	Music, Art, Writing
Home Group A: 5 students	Home Group B: 5 students	Home Group C: 5 students	Home Group D: 5 students	Home Group E: 5 students	Home Group F: 5 students

A class of 30 students is broken into six home groups with five students in each group. One student from each home group will attend each expert group and then report back to their home group.

FIGURE 6. Sample jigsaw.

References/ Additional Resources

Aronson, E. (1978). *The jigsaw classroom.* Beverly Hills, CA: Sage.
Aronson, E. (2000–2018). *The jigsaw classroom.* Retrieved from https://www.jigsaw.org
Clarke, J. (1994). Pieces of the puzzle: The Jigsaw method. In S. Sharan (Ed.), *Handbook of cooperative learning methods* (pp. 34–50). Westport, CT: The Greenwood Press.
Tomlinson, C. A. (2001). *How to differentiate instruction in mixed-ability classrooms* (2nd ed., pp. 52, 59). Alexandria, VA: ASCD.

About the Author

Laurie E. Westphal was a teacher for more than 15 years and now works as an independent gifted education consultant, educating teachers nationwide about using differentiation to meet the needs of all learners.

PRUFROCK PRESS INC.™

ISBN-13: 978-1-61821-789-9

51295

9 781618 217899